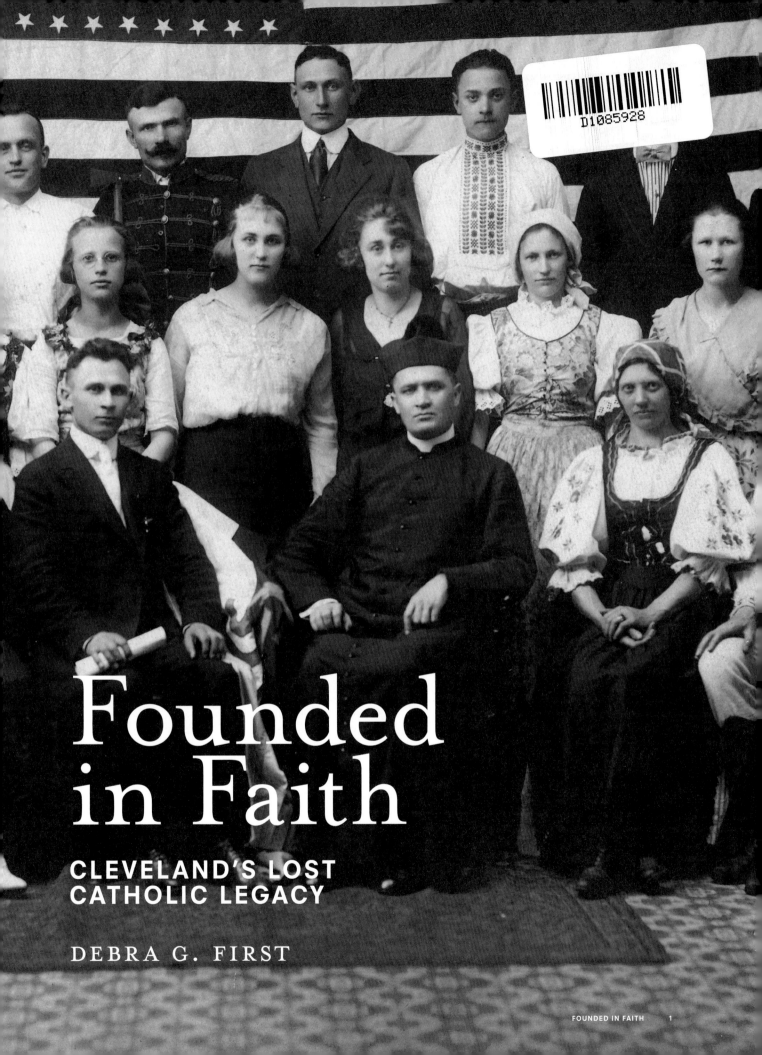

Founded in Faith

CLEVELAND'S LOST CATHOLIC LEGACY

DEBRA G. FIRST

NO MATTER WHAT ACCOMPLISHMENTS YOU ACHIEVE,
SOMEBODY HELPS YOU. **ALTHEA GIBSON**

DEDICATION
They say behind every good man is a woman,
But I know that behind every good woman is a family,
and mine is a POWERHOUSE!
I can never thank them for all that they do
and for making me the woman I am today…
they are my everything:
Ricky First
Billy First
Henry First
Jamie First
and Rick First, my husband and best friend

PUBLISHED BY
CLEVELAND LANDMARKS PRESS, INC.
13610 SHAKER BOULEVARD, SUITE 503
CLEVELAND, OHIO 44120-1592

WWW.CLEVELANDLANDMARKSPRESS.COM
216.658.4144

ISBN: 978-0-936760-28-5

LIBRARY OF CONGRESS CONTROL NUMBER:
2010929825

DESIGNED BY
TIMOTHY LACHINA
WALTER GREENE + COMPANY
CLEVELAND HEIGHTS, OHIO

PRINTED BY
BOOKMASTERS, INC.
ASHLAND, OHIO

COVER IMAGE: ST. LAWRENCE CHURCH

Debra First was graduated from the Cleveland Institute of Art in 1992 with a BFA in photography. Debbie has always been drawn to the human element, and she tries to capture its essence in her many and varied photographic projects.

She has operated her own photography business for more than 15 years, its primary focus on portraiture and architecture. Among her many projects, her architectural photography highlighting Cleveland's financial sector is featured throughout the Hyatt Hotel and Arcade in downtown Cleveland.

The idea for *Founded in Faith* was conceived upon hearing the announcement that some 50 plus parishes in the Cleveland Diocese would be merged or closed. She felt it would be important to have her family visit these churches and experience their grandeur and historic significance. As the real impact of the diocese's announcement began to settle, it became apparent that cultural heritage would be lost and that human stories and legacies would be left behind as these churches were closed. The focus of the project then became to appreciate that cultural heritage, recognizing the community of these parishes and their rich history, while also capturing the beauty of the structures themselves.

Debbie continues to pursue the human element in her photography, while she forever balances her work life and what she holds most dear—her family. Debbie lives in Cleveland Heights with her husband Rick and their four boys, Ricky, Billy, Henry, and Jamie.

ST. CASIMIR CHURCH

PREACH THE GOSPEL AT ALL TIMES, AND WHEN NECESSARY
USE WORDS.   ST. FRANCIS OF ASSISI

ST. CASIMIR CHURCH

Contents

Preface

ANY CITY GETS WHAT IT ADMIRES, WILL PAY FOR, AND, ULTIMATELY, DESERVES... AND WE WILL PROBABLY BE JUDGED NOT BY THE MONUMENTS WE BUILD BUT BY THOSE WE HAVE DESTROYED. **FAREWELL TO PENN STATION, NEW YORK TIMES EDITORIAL, OCTOBER 30, 1963**

It was my grandfather who first shared this quote with me, and it has haunted me ever since, instilling in me the great importance of tradition and history. I have always believed, and tried to instill in my children, that family is everything. We must cherish the traditions and heritage forged by our forebears, who came to Cleveland to carve out an existence for themselves and future families. A critical extension of family was the neighborhood, the pockets of ethnicity that dotted the city; and central to every neighborhood was the Church.

The Church strengthened the backbones of the families, nurtured their faith, cultivated their friendships, and enriched their sense of community. The church was where they would meet each week to pray, reflect, hope, and dream. There the beginnings of children's lives were celebrated through Baptism. There individuals became one through marriage. There they grieved loved ones who passed before them. Churches, in fact, became a part of the family — a living, breathing part that held those most dear in a close embrace.

As each generation strives to provide better for its children, the faces of neighborhoods evolve, suburbs sprout, and people migrate. While the memories of so many families are intimately linked with their church, the congregations and communities their churches serve are no longer the ethnic enclaves they once were. In 2009, Bishop Richard Lennon announced that 52 parishes in the Cleveland Diocese would be closed or merged, resulting in the closure of 29 or more churches. For many, this decision and its implications were wrenching. Many of these congregations have appealed the bishop's decision. At the time of this writing perhaps not all decisions are final, but the fate of most is imminent.

With their rich histories and well of memories, the closure of these churches, for so many, is like losing a family member.

After absorbing Bishop Lennon's announcement, it became important to me that my four boys experience these treasures before their doors were forever closed. Since I am a photographer, my husband suggested that I consider photographing each of the churches for a more permanent record of our forthcoming pilgrimage. As I thought more about it, it became clear to me that we were not just losing beautiful landmarks. Many parishioners would also be saying goodbye to their faith community, to the starting point of their family's cultural journey in our country and to memories forged over generations. Parishioners feared that they must lose their continuity with the past and its sense of heritage if forced to find new homes in other congregations.

In some way, I felt that merely photographing these churches could not do justice to the emotional losses that were imminent. I realized that it was the shattered heritage and fractured sense of community that most singularly would account for the sadness to ensue in the coming months.

I set out then not only to provide a photographic documentation of these beautiful places of worship, but also to become involved with parishioners who, as did the generations who preceded them, had worked tirelessly to maintain these communities of faith. Throughout the past year, my family and I attended Masses, picnics, pancake breakfasts, and ice cream socials at as many of these churches as possible. We met many wonderful people who generously shared their lives with us. Tears were shared at many a kitchen table over kifli or kolaczki, as the continued realization of loss was unavoidable.

I have attempted here not only to capture the beauty and grandeur of these places of worship, but also to provide a sounding board for the voices that called out from within them. Their histories poignantly recall the significant moments spent within these walls, described to me by, in some cases, generations of families who have celebrated each stage of their own lives in these now shuttered churches.

I share these histories and memories with you so that these churches will continue to be celebrated for the imprint they have left on so many lives and the undeniable role they have played in shaping and serving the neighborhoods and communities in which they once thrived.

There were six churches that closed before I could photograph their interiors. I regret that I could not share in this book these churches, with each of their individual beauties and unique styles. I did, however, photograph the exterior of each one so that they would be represented.

Eight of the churches covered here have appeals of their closings pending in Rome; the Vatican will make the final decision regarding these.

DEBRA G. FIRST
MAY 2010

ST. ADALBERT CHURCH

Introduction

"The Age of Faith" is the term often used by historians to describe the high Middle Age. Religious faith was interwoven into almost all aspects of human life. The liturgical calendar determined which days were to be celebrated and which were times for penance. Theatre arts consisted of miracle and morality plays. Veneration of the saints and their relics was a dominant theme, and pilgrimages to their shrines formed the "vacations" of the era. But probably the most lasting and still inspiring remnants from the Age of Faith are the great cathedrals that centuries later still grace the European continent.

No one would describe the last two centuries as another "age of faith." Rather it has been a period when people have looked primarily to science rather than to theology for what to believe. The powerful quest for eternal life has often taken a back seat to the more insistent pursuit of a higher standard of living, a better quality of material life.

And yet, faith has not been totally lost.

The immigrant Catholic Church of Cleveland offers clear evidence of the heritage of faith. As immigrants from Europe came to the United States in a quest for greater opportunity, they brought with them the traditions that gave them solidarity in their homelands. Their Catholic faith was central to their lives, and in their new homeland they sacrificed greatly to build their parishes, churches, and schools. The churches they built were often named after one of the saints from their native land, and the shrines within them were dedicated to these cherished models of Christian life.

The parish church was, of course, primarily a place of worship. The familiar Latin words and the Gregorian psalmody, connecting as they did with the church rituals of their former homelands, brought a sense of continuity and comfort in a land that often seemed alien. Forty Hours devotions, Corpus Christi processions, and Christmas midnight Masses were especially meaningful to the faithful. And, of course, those events which mark the way-stations of life — baptisms, marriages, funerals — bound the people to their local church.

The parish community was also a place where other aspects of the immigrants' culture were kept alive. Parish dinners and dances mirrored the festivals of the "old country." The schools were often bilingual, helping the newcomers to gain skill with English, while also helping the new generation retain their parents' native tongue. The parish was the focal point for the faithful flock's ethnicity.

It was the tide of immigration that helped Cleveland thrive at the end of the 19th and into the 20th century, and the Diocese of Cleveland thrived with it. A defining moment in the history of the Church in Cleveland came in 1935 when it hosted the Eucharistic Congress. The Congress drew 75,000 to a Saturday midnight Mass at Cleveland Municipal Stadium. On Sunday a huge crowd of

1935 EUCHARISTIC CONGRESS

CLEVELAND PRESS COLLECTION OF CLEVELAND STATE UNIVERSITY LIBRARIES

300,000 lined the route from St. John the Evangelist Cathedral to the stadium. There were 22,000 marchers in that procession, most garbed in some form of religious dress, as the Eucharist was carried to an altar set up in the stadium outfield. A throng of 125,000 crowded into the stadium for the devotions, the largest crowd ever to attend a stadium event. Such was the vibrancy of Catholic life at the time.

The last 50 years have seen marked changes in both the city and the Church. The clearest signal of the magnitude of the change came in June 2007, when Richard Lennon, bishop of Cleveland, announced a need to "downsize." The reduction in the number of parishes would come from throughout the eight-county diocese, but the greatest loss would be felt among the urban churches, especially those in the city of Cleveland, where a total of 27 were to be shuttered.

The underlying causes of this sad scenario are many, and sociologists will surely devote much time to studying them and arguing their relative impact. But certain facts cannot be ignored, and these certainly have played their role in the downsizing mandate.

Since 1950 there has been a major out-migration from the city to the suburbs and even beyond. In 1950 there were 914,808 residents in the city of Cleveland, representing 66% of Cuyahoga County's 1,389,582. As the 2010 census approaches, estimates calculate the current population of the city at 433,000, while Cuyahoga County's numbers hover around 1,301,000, a loss of some 24% since the county peak in 1970.

The Catholic population of the diocese has also shrunk by about 20% from its peak in 1970. These numbers reflect the larger national picture.

The Pew Forum on Religion & Public Life in its 2010 national study reports that 33% of those individuals who were raised as Catholics no longer describe themselves as Catholics. A further impact on the vitality of the Diocese of Cleveland is that the number of those who attend Mass regularly has fallen to just 29%, a reduction of 55% since 1970.

Accompanying these changes has been a marked decline in vocations to the Priesthood. In 1940 the number of diocesan clergy was at its peak (582), and the numbers remained relatively stable until 1970. There has been a steady drop since then, with few in seminary training for the future. The diocese has projected that there will be only 258 diocesan priests under age 70 by 2011.

Data such as these clearly contributed to the bishop's decision to downsize. Doing so will permit him to reallocate the diocese's ever-dwindling resources. The process, however, has been wrenching for all involved, and it will inevitably further destablilize inner city neighborhoods.

This book reflects on 21 of the Diocese of Cleveland's closed churches (six closed before this project could get to them). Its many beautiful photographs pay dutiful tribute to the faith that years ago built these stirring edifices for the honor and glory of God. Times indeed may change, but worthy deeds deserve to be remembered. Hopefully this book does its part to document that rich heritage of faith that marked the lives of the Catholic faithful in Greater Cleveland.

JAMES A. TOMAN
May 2010

St. Peter

SUPERIOR AVENUE AT EAST 17TH STREET, CLEVELAND
FOUNDED: 1853
FIRST MASS: 1853
LAST MASS: EASTER SUNDAY, APRIL 4, 2010

WE ABUSE LAND BECAUSE WE REGARD IT AS A COMMODITY BELONGING TO US. WHEN WE SEE LAND AS A COMMUNITY TO WHICH WE BELONG, WE MAY BEGIN TO USE IT WITH LOVE AND RESPECT. **ALDO LEOPOLD**

IN 2010 ST. PETER CHURCH WAS THE oldest Catholic Church in continuous use in the Diocese of Cleveland.

It was also one of the few pre-Civil War buildings in the city of Cleveland. The parish was created to meet the needs of the growing number of German-speaking immigrants who were settling in Cleveland. Designed by architects Heard and Porter, the church building was begun in 1857 and dedicated in October 1859 by the first Bishop of Cleveland, Amadeus Rappe.

Throughout St. Peter's 150-year history, the parish has been a strong and vibrant presence in the city during both times of growth and times of decline. For 110 years, an elementary school served thousands of children in the city. St. Peter was the original site of the motherhouse of the Sisters of Notre Dame and of Notre Dame Academy.

There are several historic pieces of art at St. Peter. The altar is the work of local sculptor Norbert Koehn. Constructed of limestone, its gothic arches echo the shapes found throughout the church. The processional cross is more contemporary in design; it is carved from linden wood, silver-leafed and set with stones. The base and staff are of hand-forged iron. Three original statues remain in the church. The Madonna and Child to the right of the altar was made in Munich, Germany, around 1865. The statues of Ss. Peter and Paul, carved in the 1860s by a local craftsman, flank the gathering area. There are 14 stained glass windows:

St. Peter receiving the keys to heaven
The Annunciation
The Nativity
The Presentation of Jesus in the temple
Jesus in the temple
The baptism of Jesus
Jesus blessing the children
Women of Samaria at the well
Gethsemane
The Resurrection
The Coronation of Mary Queen of heaven
St. Peter freed from prison
Doctors of the Church
Decorative pattern

Throughout the years, St. Peter parishioners worked hard to restore the legacy of their church by extensive renovation and restoration of the interior. The most recent project was rebuilding the church tower and belfry, the reinstallation of the historic bells, and the installation of new doors and a stained glass window. These projects restored St. Peter Church to much of its original beauty and prominence. The community of St. Peter offered a vibrant education and arts programs as well as commitment to works of service and justice. Parishioners remain proud that their efforts resulted in a rebirth of a community of faith in the heart of the city.

The parishioners are grateful to Fr. Robert Marrone who served as pastor during this time of revitalization. His vision not only led to the renovation of the church but was a key to the parishioners' outreach to the community.

After their church's doors were locked and they were no longer able to meet on the premises, many of the parishioners joined in forming the Community of St. Peter. They found meeting space elsewhere and have pledged to continue their outreach to the broader community.

St.Procop

WEST 41ST STREET, CLEVELAND
FOUNDED: 1872
FIRST MASS: SEPTEMBER 1872
LAST MASS: AUGUST 30, 2009

THE INSIGNIFICANCES OF DAILY LIFE ARE THE IMPORTANCES AND
TESTS OF ETERNITY, BECAUSE THEY PROVE WHAT REALLY IS THE
SPIRIT THAT POSSESSES US. IT IS IN OUR UNGUARDED MOMENTS
THAT WE REALLY SHOW AND SEE WHAT WE ARE. TO KNOW THE
HUMBLE MAN, YOU MUST FOLLOW HIM IN THE COMMON COURSE
OF DAILY LIFE. ANDREW MURRAY

N 1872 FOUR LOTS ON BURTON STREET were purchased for $3,200, and St. Procop parish, named in honor of the patron saint of farmers and manual craftsmen, was organized. In 1874, a two-floor church and school was built and dedicated. In June 1896, Fr. Wenceslaus Panuska became pastor. Three years later, under his leadership, the parish decided to build a grand Italian-Byzantine style church with a central dome and two towers, moving away from the predominantly Gothic-style architecture that most Cleveland churches featured at the time. The dimensions were enormous: 144 feet long with a 60-foot-wide main body, 88-foot-wide nave, and with seating for 1,300.

In 1901, Fr. Cerveny was appointed St. Procop pastor, a post he held for the next 41 years. During this time he oversaw the completion of the church by Christmas Day 1902. It was dedicated on July 4, 1903. Fr. Cerveny also oversaw the building of a four-year high school, and a new convent. He was able to keep the parish debt-free during his tenure as pastor.

In 1962, deterioration and high repair costs forced the removal of the central dome and the two towers. By 1965 change had clearly set in, and only 160 students were enrolled in the high school, forcing its closure. During the years that followed, enrollment in the grade school also declined, and in 1975 it too closed its doors.

Sadly, the dedication and generous support of the loyal St. Procop parishioners were not enough to keep the doors open to this very caring and welcoming community of faith.

It was during a recent Sunday Mass that the magnitude of devotion and loss at St. Procop presented itself. The parishioners had arranged for Sr. Deanne Zawadski to give a seminar on loss to better equip them for what they were experiencing. She challenged the parishioners to take hold of the loss and own it in their own way, on their own terms. In doing so, they could have some control over a reality they ultimately were completely powerless to change.

Sr. Deanne asked each person to go to a location within the church that held special meaning for them — the pew where they and their family always sat, or perhaps the altar where they were married or watched their children marry. At first, most simply stood and stared about the expanse of the space, searching for what might help them work through their feelings. Slowly, people began to move toward various locations and artifacts within the church, all the while silent.

An elderly man moved toward the baptismal font. He moved slowly and was careful with his footing. He touched the baptismal font and then leaned on it for support, sobbing. He said that each of his children and grandchildren had been baptized at that font. Through his tears he recalled, "We stood around this bowl and watched with such happiness as we started the lives of each and every one of them." He also buried his wife and a son from St. Procop.

He spoke softly about all that he would miss and continued, "How can anyone say goodbye to this? How can you have closure about generations of families who have grown and watched others grow in this community? I wonder what community will be there when it is my turn to say goodbye to this earth to be with those who left before me."

ANNA AND FRANK FANTA OCT. 1914   BESSIE AND ELI COTTLE JAN. 1946   MARY THERESE AND WAYNE SLOTA NOV. 1974
THREE GENERATIONS MARRIED AT ST. PROCOP

St.Stanislaus

ELYRIA AVENUE, LORAIN
FOUNDED: FEBRUARY 1908
LAST MASS: SEPTEMBER 27, 2009

THE PAST ITSELF, AS HISTORICAL CHANGE CONTINUES TO ACCELERATE,
HAS BECOME THE MOST SURREAL OF SUBJECTS—MAKING IT POSSIBLE...
TO SEE A NEW BEAUTY IN WHAT IS VANISHING. SUSAN SONTAG

OWARDS THE LATE 19TH CENTURY and the beginning of the 20th Century, thousands of Polish immigrants made their way to the United States hoping to find work. Many settled in Lorain due to its industry and the promise it held for making a living. In 1907 in "South" Lorain, 93 families asked Bishop Ignatius F. Horstmann for permission to establish a new parish. Because of the shortage of Polish-speaking priests, however, it was not until February 1908 that the first pastor was assigned. The parish received permission to borrow $40,000 to give their new parish a home site. Lots were purchased in December 1908, and the contract was awarded to Carey Construction Company to begin building the church and school.

The cornerstone was laid on August 1, 1909. The newspaper wrote that the event promised to be "one of the greatest in the history of local Catholicism." It was a day on which more than 20 clergymen led a parade of over 1,000 Cleveland visitors to the site of the new building. The first Mass was held in the partially finished upstairs on Easter Sunday, 1910.

The parish Altar and Rosary Society was organized on October 20, 1911, making it the oldest organization at St. Stanislaus. Money was tight at the time, so the pastor decided to postpone plans for a rectory, choosing instead to live at neighboring Nativity Parish. In 1916 the interior of the church was completed, and the altar, pews, Stations of the Cross, and other church furnishings were purchased.

Monthly house collections began to solve some financial problems. Social life began to flourish. Societies were organized, and plays, picnics, and other outings became frequent events for the parish. In 1920 a home was finally purchased for a rectory on Apple Avenue. A "New Church" fund began in 1929 after several lots on Elyria Avenue and East 27th Street were purchased, but building of the new church was postponed due to the depression.

The laying of the new church's cornerstone took place on October 1, 1939. It was completed and blessed by Bishop James McFadden on June 16, 1940. The old church was remodeled into a gymnasium and auditorium. Along with the new church came changing times. In 1948, the practice of reading the Gospel and delivering sermons was changed from Polish to English at several Masses. In the late 1940s a pledge drive took place for an organ and stained-glass windows. Renovations to the school and rectory started in 1951.

With increased enrollment in the school, there was need for more teaching nuns. As the convent was not large enough to house more nuns, they decided to raze the existing building and build a new convent. The ground was blessed, and construction began in 1957. Bishop Edward F. Hoban dedicated the new convent chapel on May 7, 1958.

Gradually enrollment in the school began to decrease, and in 1981 it graduated its final class. Thus began many events signaling the decline of St. Stanislaus.

The parish's 75th anniversary booklet contained the following:

The Catholic Church is changing and that means St. Stanislaus will be changing too.

As fewer ethnic people remain in the inner city, such churches will slowly become Americanized, meaning no one nationality will dominate them. And, as people move away from the cities to the placid suburbs, the inner city churches will decrease in size and perhaps be consolidated with other neighborhood churches. We see this as a very real possibility because of the shortage of vocations.

Meanwhile, it remains important for us to display our Polish heritage proudly and hold it to high esteem for all to see. For if we forget our roots, we cannot face the future with certainty.

The anniversary booklet had correctly predicted the course of events. The end came for St. Stanislaus Church in 2009. The end indeed has made it more difficult for the remaining parishioners to hold on to their heritage.

St.Adalbert

EAST 83RD STREET, CLEVELAND
FOUNDED: 1883
FIRST MASS: JANUARY 1, 1883
LAST MASS: MAY 2, 2010

WHEN WE'VE BEEN HERE TEN THOUSAND YEARS
BRIGHT SHINING AS THE SUN.
WE'VE NO LESS DAYS TO SING GOD'S PRAISE
THAN WHEN WE'VE FIRST BEGUN.

JOHN NEWTON

 **APID INDUSTRIALIZATION IN THE WEST BROADWAY NEIGHBORHOODS** surrounding St. Wenceslaus Church led a number of its Bohemian parishioners to move farther east beyond Willson Avenue (now East 55th Street). Realizing the four-mile trek to St. Wenceslaus School was too far for their children, a committee of men organized the St. Adalbert Society, which in 1882 rented space for a school in Stehlik's Hall at Garden Street and Lincoln Avenue.

The society quickly launched a fund-raising drive that drew the attention of Bishop Richard Gilmour who, on January 1, 1883, granted permission for the establishment of a church and school. Construction on a frame church and school began on September 5, 1883, the start of St. Adalbert's long history.

St. Adalbert, as it was structured in more recent times, was the result of a 1961 merger with Our Lady of the Blessed Sacrament. Our Lady of the Blessed Sacrament began after World War I when black Catholics were finding it difficult to identify with their white neighboring Catholic parishes. With help from Fr. Joseph Smith and a strong handful of men and women, they worked to establish Our Lady of the Blessed Sacrament in 1922. It began with 21 families and grew over the following year to 122 families.

By the end of the 1950s, though, the original St. Adalbert had a very small handful of aging parishioners holding onto their parish. So in 1961 Our Lady of the Blessed Sacrament merged with St. Adalbert with the promise of a school to be built. In 1969, the first black pastor in the Cleveland Diocese, Precious Blood Father Gene Wilson, was assigned to St. Adalbert.

While Fr. Wilson was at St. Adalbert Church, he commissioned a local artist to paint black the religious figures in the church. He was sensitive to his parishioners and wanted the figures to more appropriately represent his congregation. The figures were a focal point when one entered the church. One could not help but notice the statue of Moses at the top of the altar, leading his people to freedom, an image especially rich in meaning for the congregation.

Fr. Wilson left St. Adalbert in 1977 to study theology at Berkeley. He ministered in California until 2006, and then was assigned to the Sorrowful Mother Shrine in Bellevue, Ohio. In 2010 he celebrated his 82nd birthday and the 50th anniversary of his ordination to the Priesthood.

The parishioners are thankful to Fr. Wilson for his addition to the altar, as well as for his leadership and compassion throughout his extended service to St. Adalbert and its community.

Precious Blood Father Kenneth Pleiman served as the parish's final pastor, leaving only when the church was finally closed.

FR. GENE WILSON IN FRONT OF THE MAIN ALTAR AT ST. ADALBERT.

St. Francis

SUPERIOR AVENUE & EAST 71ST STREET, CLEVELAND
FOUNDED: 1887
FIRST MASS: SEPTEMBER 11, 1887
LAST MASS: OCTOBER 4, 2009

WE SHAPE OUR BUILDINGS: THEREAFTER THEY SHAPE US.
WINSTON CHURCHILL

EARS AGO, IT WAS A COMMON PRACTICE to name a church after the largest donor. In the case of St. Francis, that happened to be Anton Poelking, Sr. Since the name St. Anthony, however, had just been given to another new parish in Cleveland, the parish was named after Fr. Westerholt, who started the new parish as a mission of St. Peter Church for the east end of Cleveland's German community.

Construction on a new church building for St. Francis began in 1901; the first Mass was celebrated there two years later. The church was patterned after St. Michael's Church in Cologne, Germany. Its exterior came from stone from the old Post Office building on Cleveland's Public Square. The church was dedicated on June 26, 1904.

The parish added St. Francis School in 1907. It had 14 classrooms, an auditorium/gymnasium on the third floor, as well as a hall and kitchen in the basement. It educated both elementary and high-school students. When the high school closed its doors in June 1966, the Notre Dame Sisters continued to teach at the elementary school.

St. Francis Church was hit with tragedy on December 2, 1970, when it burned to the ground as a result of a fire that had started next door in an abandoned apartment building. Parishioners Mr. and Mrs. John Vlosich wrote at the time: "Although St. Francis Parish is more than buildings, the buildings are symbolic of the spiritual life needed in order to keep a community and city alive." On Christmas Eve that year, the members of St. Francis gathered in the basement hall of the school to celebrate Mass, the first Mass in what would ultimately become the new parish church.

Over the years as people moved to the suburbs, the parish family diminished, yet St. Francis still retained the loyalty of many. The class of 1952 is a good example – they are a small group of women, large in heart. Janet Gehring Birtley was one of those members.

She attended both the elementary school and high school. She reflects, "I wouldn't change being in this small school for any other school in the world. My classmates are the friends who have stayed with me, who have been present for every major event in my life. They have helped me, and we have enjoyed one another in our fun times and supported each other in the hardest of times."

The women of the class of 1952 still meet bi-monthly for lunch. Kay Gries Deininger graduated from the co-ed St. Francis Elementary School in 1948 and then continued at the all-girl high school. She keeps the records of addresses, phone numbers, jobs, births, and deaths that have taken place within their class.

At winter lunch gatherings, they had the custom of pulling names for a Christmas gift exchange. But as time passed, they realized they could support a larger cause, and they turned to what had influenced them all so strongly, St. Francis School. The elementary school Class of 1948 collectively gives money to the school each Christmas to provide tuition for a family that could not otherwise afford it. This gesture affords a solid educational experience and hopefully a lifetime rich in friendship and memories.

For most, the pending closure of their church brought a sense of loss. Some were unable to move past that overwhelming feeling. They felt their history of faith could not simply be transferred to another church. They feared their rich history would die when their church closed its doors forever.

There are others, though, whose thoughts focused less about loss and more about gratitude for a childhood of happy memories and a faith that continues to propel them in their actions today as adults. It has allowed them to go into the world with a spiritual richness to bring to a new generation of the faithful. They understand the changes in their neighborhood and the negative impact this evolution has had on their church, but they reflect more on the beautiful memories of a place and time that has long passed for them, for they too have moved on to different times in their lives.

ST. FRANCIS CHURCH WAS HIT BY FIRE ON DECEMBER 2, 1970.

THE CLEVELAND PRESS COLLECTION OF THE CLEVELAND STATE UNIVERSITY LIBRARIES.

CLASS OF 1948

FROM LEFT: JANET (GEHRIG) BIRTLEY
NORBERT HANNIBAL
KAY (GRIES) DEININGER

Sacred Heart of Jesus

EAST 71ST STREET & KAZIMIER AVENUE, CLEVELAND
FOUNDED: 1888
FIRST MASS: DECEMBER 25, 1889
FINAL MASS: MAY 2, 2010

ARCHITECTURE IS LIFE, OR AT LEAST IT IS LIFE ITSELF TAKING
FORM AND THEREFORE IT IS THE TRUEST RECORD OF LIFE AS IT WAS
LIVED IN THE WORLD YESTERDAY, AS IT IS LIVED TODAY OR EVER
WILL BE LIVED. FRANK LLOYD WRIGHT

UGE NUMBERS OF IMMIGRANTS
POURED INTO CLEVELAND in
the late 19th century. Cleveland was
experiencing industrial growth,
its steel industry being one of the
city's major employment draws for
the immigrants.

For most Catholic immigrants, establishing
their own church and community signaled success
in their new country. A large number of Polish
immigrants migrated from the area surrounding
St. Stanislaus down what at the time was Marcelline
Avenue (now East 71st Street) to the Brecksville
Road-Harvard Avenue area. They purchased land
on Marcelline Avenue between Krakow and Kazimier
avenues in hopes of starting their new church.

The pastor at St. Stanislaus, Fr. Anton F.
Kolaszewski, supervised the construction of the
first Sacred Heart of Jesus Church. Fr. Kolaszewski
and the Polish Catholics in the area known as "the
Orchard" celebrated their first Mass on the building's second floor church on Christmas Day, 1889.
Monsignor Felix Boff dedicated the combination
church and school on June 22, 1890. On August 6,
1891, Sacred Heart welcomed its first pastor,
Fr. Felix Orzechowski.

By 1900 the parish's fourth pastor realized
the need for a larger church, and the parish broke
ground to construct a modified Baroque-style
church with twin bell towers. The project, however,
was halted by a shortage of funds when only the
church basement had been completed. The parish
decided to use the basement for Mass, and the
original church became a social hall. During the
next three decades, the parish faced several financial crises, culminating in 1938 with the threat of
foreclosure. H. R. Templeton of the Cleveland
Trust Company came to the aid of Sacred Heart
and arranged for a loan.

The postwar era brought dramatic change
to the parish. After four decades of celebrating
Mass in the lower church, the parish finally opened
the upper church. Bishop Edward F. Hoban
dedicated the new building on May 6, 1951.

By the 1970s Sacred Heart of Jesus School
was facing an enrollment decline, and so it was
merged with that of neighboring Immaculate Heart
of Mary parish and renamed the Jesus and Mary
School.

For any parish to celebrate the present, one
must turn to the past. At Sacred Heart, the hearty
Polish immigrants who immigrated to the U.S. to
better their families' lives left their homeland
seeking relief from religious oppression, poor
economic conditions, and political dominance by
other nations. They chose Cleveland to seek that
better life. If not for their great faith, courage, and
perseverance, Sacred Heart of Jesus would not have
become the mainstay of the local community. The
people of the parish will forever be grateful for
those who forged the way.

While the history of the Sacred Heart of
Jesus has been tumultuous, the parish was a living
reminder to all of those Catholic Polish immigrants
who had worked so hard to create a piece of history
and a place of faith in Cleveland.

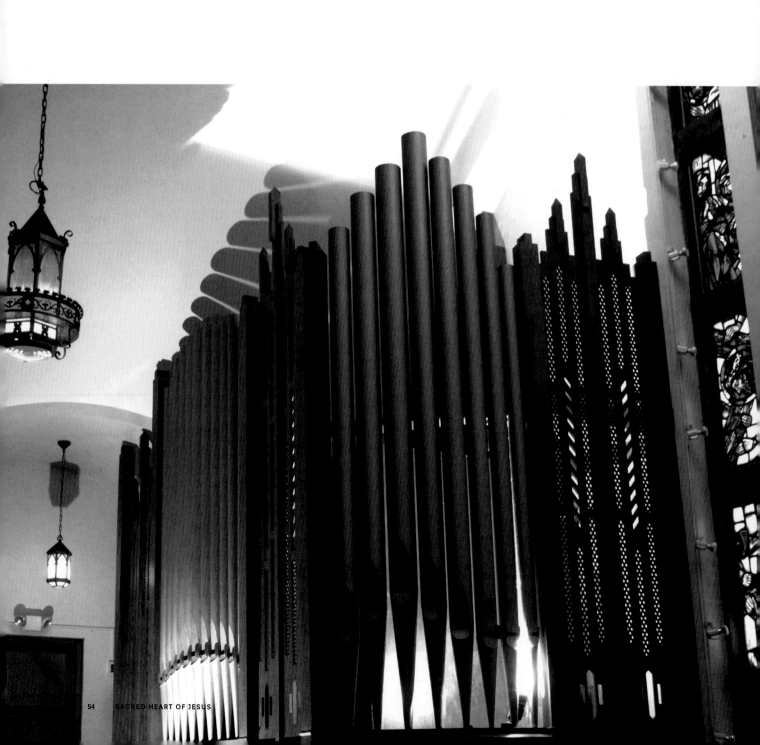

SACRED HEART OF JESUS

St.Ladislaus

EAST 29TH STREET, LORAIN
FOUNDED: 1890
FIRST MASS: JUNE 20, 1905
LAST MASS: SEPTEMBER 27, 2009

THE PRESENT IS THE EVER MOVING SHADOW THAT DIVIDES YESTERDAY WITH TOMORROW. IN THAT LIES HOPE. **FRANK LLOYD WRIGHT**

HE SHEFFIELD LAND COMPANY was created by steel giant Thomas L. Johnson to develop South Lorain. In April 1895 steel operations started there. The average wage at that time was one dollar a day, and it was a very long day.

A huge incentive for the Hungarian immigrants was that Johnson paid his workers $1.50 for a day's wage. When the Hungarians came to Lorain, they settled in what was then known as the "foreign area," between Vine and Pearl avenues. Hostility to the newcomers was quite strong, and the Sheffield Land Company promised to never sell property to foreigners. It was not until 1914 that the first parceled lots were sold to Hungarians. Despite these restrictions, to thousands of Hungarians, America was the promised land, and they kept streaming into Lorain for a better life than they had in Hungary.

At first, the Hungarians attended Mass at St. John's Church, but they were frustrated by not understanding the English sermons. They asked the bishop for a Hungarian priest. Several years later, the bishop purchased the Wood Avenue area for a new Hungarian parish — St. Ladislaus. Fr. Joseph Szabo became the first pastor at St. Ladislaus, which was then able to separate from St. John's parish.

An article in the local paper, *The Reporter*, from November 15, 1905, stated: "The structure as far as known, is the first reinforced concrete edifice to be erected in the United States and will cost $15,000." The church was to be built similar to the churches of their homeland, and the congregation wanted it to be very sturdy. Women mixed concrete, which their husbands and sons then poured into molds.

During winter weather, work on the church stalled, since at that time concrete could not be laid during cold temperatures. It took two years to complete the church building.

By 1910 the interior and exterior were complete. The altar, however, which was used until the church was closed, came in 1930. In the 1940s the stained-glass windows that illuminated the entire church on a sunny day were installed as a result of generous family donations. Their names were incorporated into the design of the windows. All debt for the parish, including the construction of church, school building, and rectory, was cancelled by January 7, 1951.

The early 1970s saw the replacement of all the church's murals. Their replacements illustrated religious life in Hungary, and included a depiction of a Corpus Christi procession through the streets of a Hungarian village.

During the 1970s and 1980s the basement was renovated to house a Hungarian Museum. Among the many cultural items on display were traditional Hungarian costumes, art, and furniture.

Fr. James Schmitz served as the last pastor of St. Ladislaus, his tenure ending only when this center of Hungarian Catholic faith was closed.

IDA BODLOR

St.Casimir

SOWINSKI AVENUE, CLEVELAND
FOUNDED: 1891
LAST MASS: NOVEMBER 8, 2009

ALL FINE ARCHITECTURAL VALUES ARE HUMAN VALUES, ELSE NOT VALUABLE. **FRANK LLOYD WRIGHT**

OR MOST CATHOLIC IMMIGRANTS entering the U.S., finding a home and a church was the first and foremost of their concerns. This was certainly true for the Polish immigrants in Cleveland. It was important not only to find a Polish-speaking church to support their spiritual needs, but also to find a hospitable neighborhood for one's traditions.

In 1891, Bishop Ignatius F. Horstmann granted permission for the founding and building of St. Casimir, making it the third oldest Polish church in Cleveland. It was situated in what was called Cleveland's Poznan neighborhood (clustered between St. Clair and Superior avenues and East 79th Street), and it became the central focus for the Polish community there.

Its first spiritual director was Fr. Peter M. Cerveny, who lived in the neighborhood and laid some of the first timbers for the church and school. He was later replaced by Fr. Stanislaw Wozny. The Felician Sisters arrived to minister to the educational needs of the parish children.

The early years were not tranquil ones for the parish. Turmoil was ever present in the parish council, and as a result, Fr. Wozny left the parish and was replaced by Fr. Francis Fremel.

On May 30, 1897, Fr. Fremel and the entire St. Casimir community celebrated the dedication of the church by Bishop Horstmann. But problems continued, culminating on the afternoon of May 14, 1911. That day disagreement turned violent when conflict arose between the supporters of newly appointed pastor Fr Piotrowski and those who opposed his decisions. The opposing camps met outside the pastor's home with deadly results. Two men were shot to death and another severely injured. The bishop stuck to his decision to keep Fr. Piotrowski at St. Casimir, but less than a year later, on March 22, 1912, Fr. Piotrowski resigned.

Many St. Casimir parishioners believe the parish's golden years began on July 4, 1924, the start of Fr. Andrew Radecki's tenure as pastor. At this point,

St. Casimir was at the peak of its parish membership, and the school was bursting at the seams with 1,200 students.

Fr. Radecki's energy and love for the people and parish brought the church to a magnificent physical and spiritual level, and it created a rich legacy for the generations which followed. He made a pilgrimage to Poland, bringing back with him on his return a copy of the miraculous picture of Our Lady of Czestochowa, Queen of Poland. It adorned the side altar of the church until the day the doors were closed.

Many other priests also left their mark on St. Casimir. The parishioners were especially happy with Msgr. Leo Telesz. He was installed as pastor on October 14, 1973. He celebrated the 70th anniversary of his ordination on October 25, 2009. Fr. Telesz was, at the time, the oldest practicing Catholic priest in the U.S.

On August 4, 1985, St. Casimir was chartered as the Solidarity Center in Cleveland. Another milestone took place on August 14 that same year, when St. Casimir was named as a historic landmark in the city of Cleveland.

Many from St. Casimir joined the religious life; 14 priests took positions in the Cleveland diocese, along with one religious brother, and 26 sisters.

Over the years, St. Casimir hosted many prominent religious figures. Among these were John Cardinal Krol, archbishop of Philadelphia, and Bishop Groblicki from Krakow, Poland. In 1975, Roman Cardinal Rubin was a guest of St. Casimir, and then from Krakow in 1969 came Karol Cardinal Wojtyla, who became Pope John Paul II in 1978.

Many families spent a lifetime at St. Casimir.

One family, a typical example of the generational loyalty of the St. Casimir flock, is the Kaminski-Sobolewski-Dragas family. Their home parish saw four generations marry and five generations join the church in Baptism:

When their church closed in 2009, many St. Casimir parishioners hoped that the decision might be rescinded. They manifested that hope and their love for their church by holding weekly prayer vigils outside its barred doors.

**KORDEYA AND
WALTER KAMINSKI**
NOV. 6, 1916

**CLARA AND
JOHN SOBOLEWSKI**
MAY 9, 1936

JOANN AND MIKE DRAGAS
NOV. 8, 1958

TAMMY AND JOHN DRAGAS
JAN. 15, 2000

FOUR GENERATIONS MARRIED AT ST. CASIMIR

St. Lawrence

EAST 81ST STREET, CLEVELAND
FOUNDED: 1901
FIRST MASS: DECEMBER 11, 1901
LAST MASS: JUNE 20, 2010

NEBESIH SEM DOMA
TO OZNAJUJETA.
NEBES SE VESELIM,
TJA PRITI SI ZELIM.

IN HEAVEN IS MY HOME,
WHERE SAINTS AND ANGELS ROAM.
HOW HAPPY I WILL BE,
AT HOME FOREVER FREE.

ANY SLOVENIAN IMMIGRANTS arriving in Cleveland in the 1880s made the Newburgh neighborhood their home. By December 1901, the Slovenian community living there had grown to 65 families, and they petitioned Bishop Horstmann for a parish of their own. Permission was given, and they celebrated their first Mass on December 11, 1901. Laying the cornerstone for a combination church and school took place on May 11, 1902. The first Mass in the new church was celebrated on August 31, 1902.

In 1923 the parish began the construction of a permanent church. The Depression caused great hardship for the people of St. Lawrence, during which a number of parishioners lost their homes. With funds in short supply, they could only afford to partially complete their church, and so they designed the basement to serve temporarily as their church. This partially completed but enclosed building served as their parish church until 1940 when the present church was constructed. On August 11,1940, the new church's altar was consecrated.

St. Lawrence is built in simplified Romanesque design, its exterior of yellow face brick trimmed with limestone. The interior walls are of yellow glazed brick, with alternating black glazed brick as accents around different focal areas. Its hand-painted wood ceiling is breathtaking. Constructed of cypress panels, it is decorated with portraits of the apostles and traditional ecclesiastical symbols, in warm colors gilt in gold. The church is cruciform in shape and seats 700 people.

One elderly parishioner remembered growing up after the Depression, when many were struggling to keep their homes while still sacrificing to get their church completed. "I remember my father going straight from the mill to the church to work night after night. We sometimes did not eat so the church could be built. It meant everything to us and our community."

As important as St. Lawrence was to the Slovenians from this community, perhaps equally important was the Slovenian home located on the same block. Nearly every Slovenian from St. Lawrence parish for 70 years has celebrated the wedding reception in its hall. For a community that has scattered throughout the Cleveland area over many decades, the Slovenian home has remained a focal point of ethnic solidarity for the Slovenian community.

As is the case with many of the other churches that also faced closure, the loss for this community goes beyond a building; it is a loss of a grounding force, a loss of community, and, in some way, a loss of heritage.

THE CHOIR AT ST. LAWERENCE

St.Wendelin

COLUMBUS ROAD, CLEVELAND
FOUNDED: 1903
LAST MASS: MAY 23, 2010

DO NOT THE MOST MOVING MOMENTS OF OUR LIVES FIND US ALL—
WITHOUT WORDS? MARCEL MARCEAU

FTER SETTLING IN OHIO CITY
during the last decade of the 19th
Century, Slovak Catholics were
challenged by language difficulties
and therefore wanted to have their
own church. They were able to
establish St. Wendelin in 1903. Under the direc-
tion of Fr. Joseph M. Koudelka, they purchased
property on Freeman Avenue and built a wood-
frame church. In 1904 the parish school was
established, served by the Notre Dame Sisters.

Opening enrollment was 100, increasing
to 1,000 by 1928.

The parish was thriving, and in 1924,
Bishop Joseph Schrembs granted permission for a
new church and school. The parish sold the property on Freeman Avenue and under the guidance of
the pastor, Fr. Augustine Tomasek, replaced it with
a new site at the corner of West 25th Street and
Columbus Road.

The beauty of the new St. Wendelin's
interior was highlighted by its "old country" flavor,
and its décor exemplified the hardworking parishioners that sacrificed so much to build it.

The next two decades brought Depression
and war, but still the community of St. Wendelin
gave generously to their church, paying off its debts
by 1943.

A meaningful example of the parishioners'
devotion to their church can be found in the person
of Agnes Gresko Dubray. In 1942, while still a
teenager, she became the church organist, the

youngest in the Diocese of Cleveland. During her
time of service, she played three weekday Masses
and three Sunday Masses, of which one was in
Slovak. She covered all the weddings and funerals,
as well as directing the parish choir. Agnes devoted
44 years of her life to the music ministry at
St. Wendelin, until her retirement in 1986.

In 1957, Fr. Tomasek was forced to retire
due to illness.

Like many other parishes of its day,
St. Wendelin enjoyed the blessings which economic
booms brought to its neighborhood. Its congregation swelled as it served as an outreach and host for
fellow Slovaks from across what is now the "Flats."
As the Slovak population grew, Our Lady of Mercy
parish was established to serve the community
living in the area that is now Tremont.

But by the 1960s change had set in, with
many parishioners relocating to the suburbs. In
1976, the school enrollment slipped to 80 students,
and St. Wendelin School was merged into the
Urban Community School. St. Wendelin, however,
continued to serve as one of the Urban Community
School campuses.

In 2002, St. Wendelin Church celebrated
its centennial, and a 100-year-old statue of
St. Wendelin, which had been in storage, was
restored and reinstalled in the church. The church
bell was also restored, and it sounded for Mass and
services. The bell fell silent with the church closing
in 2010.

Blessed Sacrament

FULTON ROAD, CLEVELAND
FOUNDED: 1903
FIRST MASS: OCTOBER 4, 1903
LAST MASS: APRIL 10, 2010

THE WORLD IS MOVED ALONG, NOT ONLY BY THE MIGHTY SHOVES OF ITS HEROES, BUT ALSO BY THE AGGREGATE OF THE TINY PUSHES OF EACH HONEST WORKER. **HELEN KELLER**

OR OVER 60 YEARS, PHYLLIS AND GEORGE ZINDROSKI dedicated their lives to the twin pillars of church and family, moving their world along with many tiny, noble pushes. As members of Blessed Sacrament, they watched their family thrive in the warm embrace of their parish. Along the way, they baptized their two children, seven grandchildren, and three great-grandchildren at the church.

The Zindroskis devoted countless hours to their parish, like many other parishioners who shared their values of family and faith. Phyllis worked in the mobile unit at the school, tutoring children of all ages. She was Altar Rosary president, and over the decades, cooked hundreds of church meals. At one time, George served as president of the Holy Name Society, and their daughter Annetta was president of the Parent Teacher Unit. Everyone knew that just one call to the Zindroski family covered all the lines of communication for both the church and school.

But over the years, Phyllis recalled wistfully, enrollment in the school dwindled as parishioners moved away to the suburbs, and Blessed Sacrament School ceased to be in 2002. Ultimately, the church, too, was forced to close its doors. Phyllis ended her years of volunteering for the church as the person who took care of the church laundry, cleaning and pressing all the altar linens and robes. She took endless pride in each fold and press, every step methodical and performed with care for the particular way Fr. Matthew Ischay liked it done. She reflected through tears, "I guess my last act of volunteering will be to receive an empty laundry basket." This humble task will mark the end of her long—and noble—history with Blessed Sacrament.

Blessed Sacrament celebrated its first Mass on October 4, 1903, and the school opened a year later to 110 children. By 1940, the student body had soared to 480 children, and the church served its burgeoning congregation with outstretched arms. For more than half a century, the parish thrived. Under Fr. Edward Hannon, the rectory was modernized in the 1950s to match the brick façade of the church.

Blessed Sacrament celebrated its Golden Jubilee on December 8, 1953, with Archbishop Edward F. Hoban dedicating the Romanesque-style church. But as Cleveland struggled through the tumultuous 1960s, Blessed Sacrament faced its own challenges. The newly built Interstate 71 wreaked havoc on the parish's residential community, uprooting many parishioners and relocating them to far-off suburbs. In 1978, Blessed Sacrament celebrated its Diamond Jubilee under the watchful eye of Fr. John Cregan.

As the neighborhood continued to evolve, the church sorrowfully bade farewell to the Humility of Mary Sisters, ending a lifetime of service that the sisters had given to the school. In 1987 Blessed Sacrament received Fr. Matthew Ischay, its final pastor, who reluctantly oversaw the closing of the school just five years later. He was also the one to see the doors of Blessed Sacrament close forever after 107 years of faithful service to the diocese and the community.

**PHYLLIS AND GEORGE ZINDROSKI LOOKING AT THEIR
WEDDING ALBUM**

St.Emeric

WEST 22ND STREET, CLEVELAND
FOUNDED: 1904
FIRST MASS: NOVEMBER 1904
LAST MASS: JUNE 30, 2010

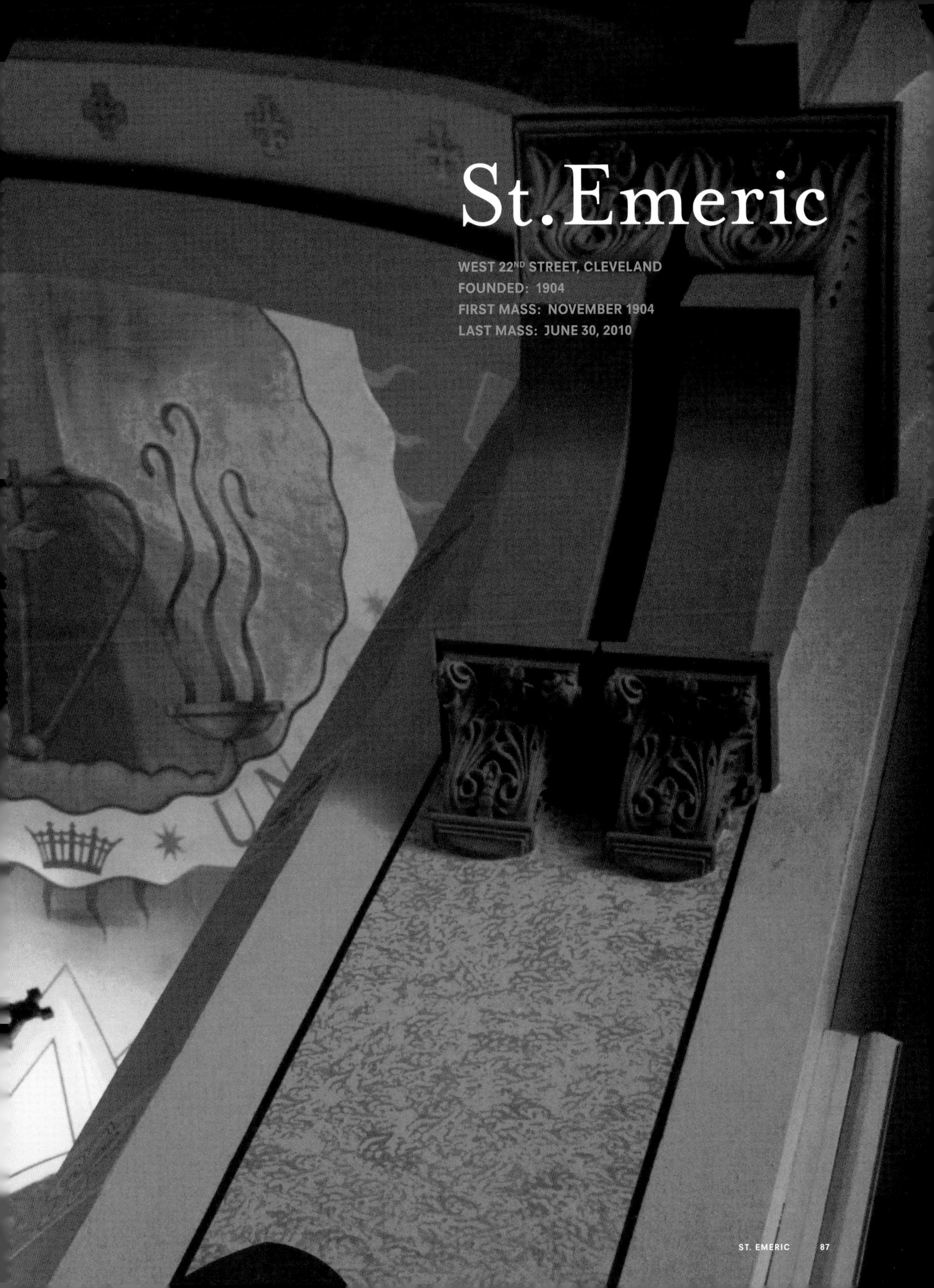

PLURIBUS ✶ UNUM

SUDDENLY, IT BECOMES A SUBVERSION OF PROGRESS TO ASSERT
THE COMMONSENSIBLE PRINCIPLE THAT COMMUNITIES EXIST FOR
THE HEALTH AND ENJOYMENT OF THOSE WHO LIVE IN THEM, NOT
FOR THE CONVENIENCE OF THOSE WHO DRIVE THROUGH THEM,
FLY OVER THEM, OR EXPLOIT THEIR REAL ESTATE FOR PROFIT.

THEODORE ROSZAK

 **HE ONGOING QUEST TO IMPROVE**
one's environment often translates
into building things that are
larger and more complex. Often
these efforts result in erasing
those elements that were the really
important pillars of the past. Sometimes, bigger
and grander is not the way. Sometimes, it is the
simple, quiet, humble places that are important.
Sometimes less really is more.

Under the guidance and with the help of
Fr. Joseph Hirling, St. Emeric parish was established. It started out in a small business building
located at 60-62 Hicks Street, later named West
24th Street. St. Emeric was established with 162
families and 432 single people. On January 22,
1905, Bishop Ignatius Horstmann dedicated a
wood-frame church, and on that same date, the
Blessed Virgin Mary Society was established,
making it the parish's oldest society.

There were several events that brought
change to St. Emeric. One of the most devastating
was a fire on February 17, 1915, which damaged the
church beyond repair. As an alternative to building
a new church, the people of St. Emeric moved just a
block away, by purchasing the old Annunciation
Catholic Church, commonly referred to as the
"Old French Church."

St. Emeric completed purchase of its new
home and its rectory in 1916 and immediately

started making necessary repairs. Sadly, fire struck
a second time on July 21, 1921, destroying the
school and badly damaging the church.

In 1924 St. Emeric became historically
connected to the Terminal Tower development.
The church property was needed for the railroad
right of way to the new downtown union station.
To achieve their need, the Van Sweringen brothers,
through their Cleveland Union Terminal Company, purchased St. Emeric Church.

In 1925 a new St. Emeric church and
school were built at its third and present location,
1860 West 22nd Street, next to the West Side Market,
overlooking downtown Cleveland. The parishioners
were able to save the altar from the "Old French
Church," bringing it to the new building; the altar
dates from the 1870s.

Over the years many improvements were
undertaken. In 1944 the interior of the church was
repainted for the first time. The murals in the
sanctuary were completed by W. A. Krusoe, a
Hungarian artist. The interior was restored again
in 1972, as the altar and sanctuary were renovated
and updated. In 2004 St. Emeric celebrated its
Jubilee year with a series of events that took place
throughout the course of that year.

Just six years later, St. Emeric parish life
was sadly brought to its end by the diocesan downsizing process.

St.Barbara

DENISON AVENUE, CLEVELAND
FOUNDED: 1905
FIRST MASS: 1905
LAST MASS: MAY 9, 2010

YOU MUST NOT LOSE FAITH IN HUMANITY. HUMANITY IS AN OCEAN; IF A FEW DROPS OF THE OCEAN ARE DIRTY, THE OCEAN DOES NOT BECOME DIRTY. **MAHATMA GANDHI**

 SMALL GROUP OF POLISH CATHOLICS, living near Henninger Road in South Brooklyn, formed St. Barbara Parish in 1905. Almost immediately, numbers of Polish families joined the parish from across the Cuyahoga River Valley in the East Denison vicinity. The community first celebrated Mass at Our Lady of Good Counsel Church, and later at the firehouse on West 23rd Street and Broadview Road.

As soon as it could afford it, the parish purchased land at Valley Road and Elston Avenue and began construction of a new church. On Christmas Day 1907, the parishioners celebrated the first Mass in their new building, which, along with the church, contained a hall and a pastoral residence.

St. Barbara, like many parishes, had an ebb and flow of both easy and difficult times as the Great Depression and migration to the suburbs hit this small church. The largest blow to this congregation, however, took place with the building of I-71 and then the Jennings Freeway next to St. Barbara's front door. This encroachment into the neighborhood forced several square blocks of families to move. They had to sell their homes to the State of Ohio's Department of Transportation. As a result, many of these families moved a distance away from the parish. The highways also set into place physical boundaries that further reduced the neighborhood from which St. Barbara drew parishioners.

One of the many to lose a home as a result of the urban expansion was the Dziedzina family. Christine Dziedzina, an only child and, until the

end, an active parishioner at St. Barbara, bitterly remembers losing her family home. Once adjacent to the church property, it became a grassy lot next to the church parking area.

She remembers the battle parishioners fought to have the planned Jennings right of way moved to save their church. Urged on by the Diocese of Cleveland, they became a concerted coalition, and after much letter writing, they were able to achieve their goal. Its intended course was adjusted, and the freeway was built and opened to traffic on December 8, 1989. Saving St. Barbara from demolition was a huge success for the parishioners as well as the diocese. Saving it in 1989 made today's decision to close the church that much more difficult for the people of St. Barbara. It had been closed by the same people who asked them to fight for its existence 21 years earlier.

In the empty lot that was once the Dziedzina home, all that remains is a portion of their fence. Christine Dziedzina can still recall the mothers of the neighborhood talking over fences like these, as well as the vegetable gardens, the front porches, and the block parties that marked summer after summer.

Chris is deeply grateful for her childhood. "They just don't have places like that one anymore. When you feel abandoned by the people who promised to protect you, you do end up feeling as if there is no one to keep you safe. When all that you were and all that you remember of things that were of utmost importance are gone, what is left to frame your story?

"What is left that says I lived here, and I made an impact... what will be left to share with the next generations?"

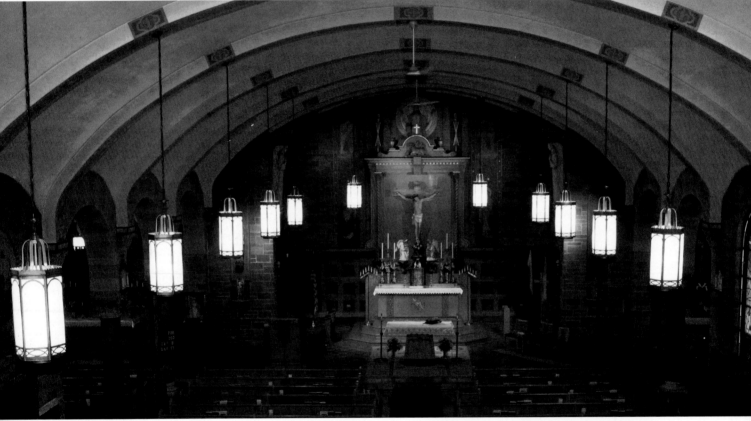

**CHRISTINE DZIEDZINA WITH HER
FIRST COMMUNION PHOTO**

St. Hyacinth

FRANCIS AVENUE & EAST 61ST STREET
FOUNDED: 1906
FIRST MASS: DECEMBER 20, 1906
LAST MASS: SEPTEMBER 9. 2010

ARCHITECTURE IS TO MAKE US KNOW AND REMEMBER WHO WE ARE.
GEOFFREY JELLICOE

LEVELAND IN THE 1870s was one of the leading manufacturing cities in the Midwest. Over time, more Polish immigrants were arriving in Cleveland eager to begin new lives. Like many other industrial areas in the late 1800s, Cleveland was overflowing with an immigrant population competing for available jobs. In the area just north of the rolling mills, though yet undeveloped in 1881, Polish settlers carved out their own community around what was to become the location for the city's first Polish church, St. Stanislaus Church, on Tod Street (now East 65th Street) and Forman Avenue.

The St. Stanislaus area was know as "Warszawa" and St. Stanislaus was considered the mother parish for the Poles. From Harvard and Ottawa roads to as far as East 71st Street and Grant Avenue, the area was called "Krakow." The residents in this area purchased small plots of property and worked in the Warszawa industrial district. Many Poles in this area also farmed and kept poultry. It was said that the roaming, hissing geese would often chase people as they passed by. As a result, the area earned the additional nickname of "Goosetown."

Another Polish community called "Jackowo" (pronounced "Yahts-Ko-vo,") grew out from this area and to the north. Many in this district worked at the Empire Plow Company, or in the other industries that lined the edge of Kingsbury Run.

The residents of the growing Jackowo in time petitioned for a new church of their own. They offered two reasons for their request: overcrowding at St. Stanislaus and the distance they had to travel to get to church. Bishop Horstmann, on December 20, 1906, granted them their new parish — St. Hyacinth (Jacka in Polish). For its first year, the services were conducted at St. Lawrence Church.

The congregation bought about ten lots at East 61st and 63rd streets which would hold the church, school, and rectory. The land cost $10,000, the church and school buildings another $20,000, and the rectory

$6,000. The cornerstone was blessed on August 4, 1907, and Mass was celebrated in the new building on Christmas that same year.

On August 23, 1908, Rt. Rev. Paul Rhode, the first American Bishop of Polish descent, dedicated and blessed the church. In 1920 the parish purchased nine additional lots for $10,000. There was no sisters' home, so therefore in 1920 a central heating plant combined with a convent was built. Due to overcrowded conditions in the school building, in 1925, an auditorium and six additional classrooms were built.

As the parish community continued to expand, the church soon proved to be too small. It was also discovered that elderly parishioners found it difficult to climb the many stairs to reach the church. In 1949 the parish asked architect Paul J. Ellsworth Potter to submit a building plan. At a cost of $150,000, in January 1950 Archbishop Edward F. Hoban approved the erection of the new church. It was finished in May 1952.

Since the start of St. Hyacinth until the closing Mass, the church had only four dedicated priests to watch over the congregation: Dr. Ludwik Redmer, 1906 to 1920; Rt. Rev. Msgr. Joseph M. Sztucki, 1920 to 1957; Rev. Joseph C. Rutkowski, 1957 to 1973; and Rev. John S. Deka, 1973 to 2001.

With the enrollment of the parish at only 200 families the church could no longer have a resident pastor. The day-to-day operation and ministry was given to Rev. Mr. Kenneth J. Piechowski, the Parish Life coordinator. Kenneth was a graduate of St. Hyacinth grade school in 1962, and he and his wife Linda were married at St. Hyacinth in 1968.

Fr. Theodore Marszal, pastor of Ss. Peter and Paul Parish in Garfield Heights was given the title of presbyteral moderator of the parish. In this role he oversaw the pastoral ministry of St. Hyacinth parish and was available for any priestly ministry that the parish needed.

The parish continued this way until the doors closed on St. Hyacinth Church in September 2009.

St.James

DETROIT AND GRANGER AVENUES, LAKEWOOD
FOUNDED: 1908
FIRST MASS: JULY 5, 1908
LAST MASS: EASTER SUNDAY 2010

TRUST, RELYING ON GOD HAS TO BEGIN ALL OVER AGAIN EVERY DAY AS IF NOTHING HAD YET BEEN DONE. **C. S. LEWIS**

N 1906, APPROXIMATELY 60 FAMILIES petitioned Bishop Ignatius F. Horstmann for a parish to be built in the western part of Lakewood Village to serve the Catholic community there. The bishop granted the parishioners' petition, and he appointed Fr. Michael Leahy St. James's first pastor. The new pastor promptly secured an empty storeroom in the O'Donnell block on Detroit Avenue where the community celebrated its first Mass on July 5, 1908. Before acquiring property on Granger and Detroit avenues in March 1912, the parish celebrated Mass in Miller Hall, located at Belle and Detroit avenues.

The parish began building its first church in June 1913. Completed within a year, the church was dedicated by Bishop John P. Farrelly on November 8, 1914. The Bishop characterized the role of the church building for the people in the parish:

"This is your house, your home. This is the place where you are to acquire strength for the lives you live. Here birth, marriage, and death will bring you."

During the next decade, membership increased, and the parish laid the cornerstone for a new building on August 30, 1925. Designed in a Sicilian-Romanesque style, it was modeled after the Cathedral of Monreale in Palermo, Italy. The bishop granted Fr. Leahy a budget of $265,000 to contract for the church's 18 marble columns. The altar was acquired for $42,000.

The Great Depression hit the construction timetable hard, and it nearly doubled the time required for completion. The new St. James Church was dedicated by Bishop Joseph Schrembs on May 21, 1935. Although the new church was built during the tumultuous Depression period, its scale, quality of materials, and complexity of design did not reflect those lean years. Rather, they served as a monument to the tenacity and persistence of its founding pastor, Fr. Leahy, and of its dedicated parishioners.

In the February 24, 1983, issue of the Lakewood Sun Press, an elder of St. James wrote:

"Father Leahy was adamant about what he wanted done and scrutinized the work every step of the way. He would climb up on the scaffolding clear to the rafters to check and see if the masons, painters, and artists were doing their work right. Heaven help them if they weren't. He was a purist who would brook no compromise."

In recognition for all that he did for St. James and his service to the Cleveland diocese, Pope Pius XI elevated Fr. Leahy to the rank of domestic prelate in 1936. Msgr. Leahy remained at St. James until his death in 1941.

The church's three sets of massive bronze doors were made by the Taylor Company in Cleveland at a cost of $6,450. There are two bell towers, followed by the bell chamber. The bells, cast with a decorative surface pattern, were made by the Petit and Fritsen Company of Holland and installed at St. James on May 16, 1955. The two bell towers terminate in a stone dome, crowned with a ring of inlaid tile, and they are marked on four sides by subtly recessed, eight-pointed stars, a church symbol commonly used to represent regeneration and Resurrection.

The St. James interior has not changed since its iconographic 1944 painting scheme. In this country, any building left alone in its original form for more than 50 years seems rare. This is especially important for St. James, because the color palette, and even the light from outside, were all calculated to create an atmosphere that transcends the ordinary. One only has to walk around the outside or step into its interior to recognize that the Church of St. James is an edifice worthy of preserving. It is a distinctive part of Greater Cleveland's — and the nation's — architectural heritage.

Much has been written on the structure of St. James. The marble and stone work is fascinating. Joseph T. Hannibal of the Cleveland Museum of Natural History has identified three types of stone columns in the church. Eight of the columns are made from Porta Santa (Holygate) marble, six are made from light Verona Red marble, and four are Red Levanto marble. The carved capital tops of the columns are said to be Rosato rose-colored marble. It is possible that the Porta Santa pillars are reused antique pillars, manufactured in the days of the ancient Romans and, only much later, purchased on the antiquities market in Italy for use in this church.

St. Hedwig

MADISON AVENUE, LAKEWOOD
FOUNDED: 1905
LAST MASS: JANUARY 17, 2010

REAL GENEROSITY TOWARDS THE FUTURE LIES IN GIVING ALL TO
THE PRESENT. **ALBERT CAMUS**

HE FIRST POLISH CATHOLICS TO ARRIVE IN LAKEWOOD, OHIO, began settling around 1890 and lived near Madison Avenue and West 117th Street. Many came from similar backgrounds and interacted with one another daily at the National Carbon Company. Over the next three years, the Polish population grew rapidly.

In December 1909, Bishop John P. Farrelly responded to the request of the Polish community to have its own nationality parish, and he established St. Hedwig, appointing Fr. Thomas Czarkowski as the church's first pastor. The community soon purchased property on Madison Avenue between Halsted and Dowd avenues and began construction of a wood-frame church. Fr. Charles Ruszkowski first dedicated St. Hedwig Church on August 6, 1914.

In 1926, the original church was replaced by a combination church and school building. The original wood structure became the parish hall. Guided by the work and loyalty of Fr. Ruszkowski, the parish community worked endlessly to overcome an almost impossible financial crisis. Fr. Ruszkowski stayed at St. Hedwig until September 4, 1957, when he was named pastor of St. Hyacinth Church.

St. Hedwig's third and final church was dedicated the on June 1, 1975. Improvements, though, continued. The parish installed a beautiful mosaic mural of St. Hedwig to adorn the sanctuary, as well as Nativity and Resurrection murals on the ceiling. New mosaic stations of the cross replaced the originals. Bavarian hand-carved wooden statues were commissioned, and a granite statue of St. Hedwig was installed in the front of the church. A new quarry tile floor replaced the original.

The parish school at St. Hedwig began in 1927 in the combination church and school building on Madison Avenue and Halstead Street. The Sisters of St. Joseph, Third Order of St. Francis, were the teachers.

Richarda Ksiazek Jambrozy was a student at St. Hedwig from 1936 until she graduated in 1944. She remembers the four classrooms on the upper floor. Only three were used for classrooms, while the fourth was partitioned off into living quarters for the sisters. One classroom served grades one through three, with several younger children coming in for afternoon kindergarten class. The second classroom served grades four through six and the third held the seventh and eighth grades, whose students were taught by the principal. In 1942, 62 children attended St. Hedwig School.

Statistics, however, can never capture the daunting job the sisters had in teaching two or three grades in each classroom, not to mention the parents' desire also to have the Polish language taught to their children. The sisters did all that and also passed along the many beautiful Polish hymns and traditions.

"Our school was quite small and was often looked down on by other bigger Catholic schools in Lakewood. Many of our graduates, though, went on to earn advanced degrees and become successful. I have always been very proud to have been a part of St. Hedwig School," reflected Jambrozy.

In 1950, a home was purchased for the sisters, allowing the school to utilize all four classrooms for teaching. Eventually, due to escalating operation costs and declining enrollment, St. Hedwig was forced to close its school in 1968. Fr. Edmund Kaczmarski was the pastor at the time of the closing, which weighed heavily on him. He fell ill, and passed away on February 5, 1973.

On July 5, 1973, Fr. John Bryk became the new pastor at St. Hedwig, and with his diligent effort and guidance the new church was started and improvements continued.

The end for St. Hedwig Church came in January 2010.

St.Cecilia

KINSMAN ROAD AND EAST 152ND STREET, CLEVELAND
FOUNDED: 1915
FIRST MASS: JUNE 12, 1915
LAST MASS: APRIL 25, 2010

RICHES AND POWER ARE BUT GIFTS OF BLIND FATE, WHEREAS
GOODNESS IS THE RESULT OF ONE'S OWN MERIT. **HELOISE OF ABELARD**

HE FIRST MASS FOR ST. CECILIA
took place in the home of the
Lyons Family on East 139th Street
on November 19, 1913. As more
families joined the parish, services
were moved to Gannon's Flour
and Feed store. Land was then purchased for
St.Cecilia Church at 152nd Street and Kinsman
Road, and a white frame church with the uncompli-
cated lines of colonial architecture took shape.

On June 12, 1915, the modest frame structure, with a seating capacity of 450, was dedicated.
The first pastor was Reverend John T. Farrell. His
rectory was a small farm house, later enlarged, which
remained the rectory to the present time.

St. Cecilia parish was identified in the
records of the diocese as being a "pentecostal
mission," meaning many nationalities worshiped
there. Italians, Germans, Poles, Irish, Bohemians,
Hungarians, and even Japanese worshipped together in what was an extraordinary blending of nationalities for those times. That spirit of the essential
oneness of all men and women lived on. St. Cecilia
remained a congregation where racial integration
was an actuality rather than an ideal.

St. Cecilia reached into two cities – Cleveland and Shaker Heights. As those cities grew,
St. Cecilia grew as well. Soon, the simple white
frame church was no longer big enough for its
expanding congregation. A new brick structure was
designed by architect Joseph Miller and built over
the standing original structure. The new St. Cecilia
church was dedicated by Bishop James McFadden on
June 17, 1942. It was able to seat 1,000 parishioners, more than doubling its original capacity.

St. Cecilia's essence has remained the same.
Through changes of time, community, families,
and faces, it has remained a welcoming house of
God, a place to receive support and blessings, and a
part of a community of believers.

Tom and Liz Walker are a couple of the
"originals" of St. Cecilia. Married more than 50
years ago at the St. Cecilia altar, they have been
sitting in the same pew every Sunday for more than
50 years. They credit the wonderful community at
St. Cecilia as an anchor through rough times and
their venue for celebration through the good.
Barbara Ann Robinson was another long-time
parishioner at St. Emeric and then at St. Cecilia,
and she has been very active in the Cleveland diocese.

When parishioners were asked to "map" the
St. Cecilia way, many spoke out about what it was
like finding their home at St. Cecilia's:

St. Cecilia was a community of warmth and
hospitality where people found genuine care,
mutual respect, and acceptance. Our relationship to
God was reflected in our bonds with each other.
The sign of peace introduced an opportunity for
fellowship, Eucharist, and forgiveness.

As one parishioner commented, "At St.
Cecilia I found a place like no other... people
wrapped their arms around you at the sign of peace
and sang with all they had, strong and loud. You
always left St. Cecilia feeling much better than you
did when you entered. You genuinely wanted to
spread that feeling to the world."

It will be hard to duplicate the spirit of inclusion
that was so much a part of the St. Cecilia legacy.

St.Margaret of Hungary

ALEXANDER ROAD, ORANGE VILLAGE
FOUNDED: 1921
FIRST MASS: DECEMBER 15, 1921
LAST MASS: NOVEMBER 1, 2009

DEAR ST. MARGARET'S, OUR ST. MARGARET'S
WE RESPOND TO HIGHEST PRAISE
TOGETHER IN JOY AND GRIEF
THY BLESSED NAME WE REVERE.

IN FAITH AND LOVE AND GRATITUDE
WE ARE GRATEFUL ONE AND ALL,
THOU SHALT FIND US E'ER DEVOTED
TO THY SPIRIT AND THY ALL!

 HE HISTORY OF ST. MARGARET OF HUNGARY began in 1922, when the fledgling parish used the facilities at Our Lady of Peace to conduct a mission for the benefit of the new church. A bishop from Hungary, Louis Shwoy, and Professor Michael Marczell of St. Emeric's College, helped raise donations, which were carried in a large soup kettle to a council member's home.

Those donations made it possible to build two small wooden buildings on East 116th Street near Buckeye Road. They were completed in 1922. One served as a church, and the other smaller building was used as a recreation hall. In that same year, the church started its catechism classes for the parish. The Social Mission Sisters of the Holy Ghost provided the guidance and, during the following three years, instructed over 600 children.

On a very hot day on June 28, 1924, the sacrament of Confirmation was administered to 375 children. That number was never surpassed in the history of the parish.

In November 1928, Fr. Andrew Koller assumed duties at St. Margaret. He was faced with much-needed repairs of the well-used wooden church and hall, both of which were too small for the large and growing congregation.

On July 28, 1926, the mortgage for the two wooden structures was paid in full to the Union Trust Company. Bolstered by a starting loan of $200,000, in 1928 the parish held a groundbreaking for a new church and school. Additional expenses covering architectural fees, landscaping, and furnishings were acknowledged by the bank, and an additional loan of $10,000 was granted.

Completed in June 1930, the new church and school floor plan were unique in that the church entrance was intersected by the school to form a crucifix. Fr. Koller entrusted the education of the children to the religious order of the Daughters of the Divine Redeemer (now called Sisters of the Divine Redeemer). Sr. Theresa was the first principal of the new school, and, after only

three years, the original ten classrooms were bursting at the seams.

On June 18, 1940, Fr. Koller broke ground for Our Lady of Perpetual Help Shrine on the property of the Divine Redeemer Home for the Aged at 4680 Lander Road in Orange Village. Unknown at the time, this location would eventually become the next site for St. Margaret of Hungary Church. On January 15, 1965, after 55 years of dedicated service, Msgr. Koller retired and received the title of pastor emeritus. Msgr. Koller passed away on January 8, 1972, at the age of 85 after 62 years of service to the Lord.

On August 23, 1972, Fr. Ladislaus Rosko, an assistant at the church since October 1965, was appointed administer of St. Margaret Church.

June 1977 marked the last graduating class of St. Margaret School. Over the years it had graduated over 2,000 students to many callings in life.

In February 1989, Bishop Anthony Pilla granted permission for St. Margaret of Hungary Church to proceed with the sale of its East 116th Street property; parishioners began to relocate the parish to the Lander Road site. The final Mass for the 116th Street location was on August 13, 1989, nearly 70 years to the day that the first Mass was celebrated there.

On March 17, 1991, St. Margaret hosted an open house at the new Lander Road location, the first time parishioners were able to set foot in the new building. Bishop Pilla dedicated the building on September 20, 1992. Over 800 parishioners and friends were in attendance.

St. Margaret of Hungary celebrated its Diamond Jubilee on November 3, 1996 with Bishop Pilla as the primary celebrant.

The Lander Road site for St. Margaret's Church proved temporary, lasting only 18 years. The parish flock had dispersed throughout the area, and the new location meant too great a commute for most of them.

Fr. Rosko remained at St. Margaret of Hungary until the final Mass was celebrated, marking him only the sixth priest of St. Margaret, celebrating 45 years at the church.

Our Lady of Mercy

WEST 11TH STREET, CLEVELAND
FOUNDED: 1922
FIRST MASS: JANUARY 10, 1922
LAST MASS: MAY 9, 2010

I SEE YOU IN A THOUSAND PAINTINGS,
MARY, SO TENDERLY DEPICTED
YET NONE OF THEM CAN BEGIN TO SHOW
YOU AS MY SOUL SEES YOU.

I ONLY KNOW THAT THE WORLD'S CHAOS
HAS SUDDENLY VANISHED LIKE A DREAM,
AND A HEAVEN OF INEFFABLE SWEETNESS
HAS OPENED FOREVER IN MY SOUL.

NOVALIS

 **UR LADY OF MERCY WAS ESTABLISHED** in 1922 by Slovak Catholics living in the Tremont community in Cleveland. While Fr. Francis Dubosh was pastor of Our Lady of Mercy, he built a brick school and turned an existing house into a convent for the Notre Dame Sisters. In 1927, Father John W. Krispinski came to Our Lady of Mercy and, saying goodbye to the Sisters of Notre Dame in 1935, welcomed teachers from Vincentian Sisters of Charity to the school. In 1948, the church found itself debt free.

The school hall was used as a temporary church to allow time for a new church to be built. On October 23, 1949, Bishop Edward F. Hoban dedicated the new, modern Romanesque-style church, a style widely used in Slovak church architecture. Our Lady of Mercy's façade is made from orchard crab stone from Tennessee. No longer quarried, it is said never to discolor. It is the same stone as that used for St. John the Evangelist Cathedral downtown, the only other church in Cleveland made from this stone.

Along the walls are stained-glass windows depicting the life of Mary. The breathtaking windows commanded attention the moment one entered the church. They were made of free-form leading and selective hand-made glass, rich in color. The windows transmitted a great deal of light, creating a warmth that radiated throughout the whole church. The windows were made in New York by a European artisan. Another noteworthy fact regarding these windows was that the image for the Dormition of Mary was depicted alongside that of her Assumption into heaven, a rare portrayal.

The character of the Church was traditional Slovak, many of the designs taken from peasant decorations. All the figures were hand-carved wood. The visual high point of the sanctuary was a large mosaic behind the altar, depicting Our Lady of Mercy holding the Christ Child. It was made of Venetian glass from Italy. Mary is the patroness of the people of Slovakia, further enhancing the Slovak heritage within the Church.

Our Lady of Mercy had many priests who helped mold its history, but none more influential than Fr. Andrew P. Laheta, a son of the parish, who attended Our Lady of Mercy grade school and celebrated his first Mass at OLM in 1943. Fr. Laheta started his service at an early age as an altar boy at Our Lady of Mercy in 1931. He was the priest at Our Lady of Mercy from 1964 until his retirement in 1988, having served at the church for 24 years.

Linda Carnivale and her nine classmates were the last graduating class of Our Lady of Mercy school before its closure in 1972; Fr. Laheta officiated. The classmates remember him with the same love and respect they have for the parish and its school. Linda speaks openly about the permanent mark Fr. Laheta left on her and her classmates' memories. For Linda, Fr. Laheta and Our Lady of Mercy were synonymous.

The Tremont neighborhood epitomized the "melting pot." Our Lady of Mercy was an extension of the neighborhood and embraced its diversity. Linda recalls, "We never saw color, race, or financial discrepancies among our classmates, not ever. We were a small class, and we never left one another's side. We continued on to different high schools, but after graduation, we were still the Class of 1972 from Our Lady of Mercy. Even now, we stay in touch, and I don't know how many classes can say that — Our Lady did that for us.

"When we were in school at Our Lady, it was our entire life," Linda says passionately. "Our families and the neighborhood... that was our whole world. We can still drive through the old neighborhood and point out which friend lived where, and we still know where they moved and where they are now. We stuck together; we looked out for one another. It's not like that now for kids. I can't go anyplace without bumping into someone I know or someone who has some kind of connection to Our Lady," says Linda. "We were a small parish that somehow seemed to touch the whole world. How many places can say that?"

FOUNDING MEMBERS OF OUR LADY OF MERCY

FR ANDREW LAHETA AS AN ALTER BOY (1ST ROW 4TH FROM LEFT)

FR LAHETA WITH LAST GRADUATING CLASS FROM OLM CLASS OF 1972

Epiphany

UNION AVENUE AND EAST 120TH STREET, CLEVELAND
FOUNDED: 1944
FIRST MASS: JANUARY 6, 1944
LAST MASS: MAY 24, 2009

STAR OF THIS STORMY SEA...
TURN YOUR HEART TO THE TERRIFYING SQUALL
IN WHICH I FIND MYSELF,
ALONE,WITHOUT A MAP.

PETRARCH

PIPHANY PARISH CELEBRATED ITS FIRST MASS on January 6, 1944, in the Novak Hall on East 130th Street and Union Avenue. Later, the Social Mission Sisters and diocesan seminarians began religious education classes in a second set of stores located on East 126th Street and Kinsman. On Christmas Eve 1947, the Epiphany community gathered to celebrate the first Mass in what was to be its final church, located at 11901 Oakfield Avenue. During the 1970s, Epiphany had an enormous presence in the Mount Pleasant area, including religious education for children and adults alike, prayer and Bible study, the Thea Bowman Center, a day-care center, and an Industrial Power Sewing Training center for employment.

In the next decade, the church and community struggled. Fr. Daniel L. Begin was appointed parish administrator in May 1982 and was named pastor the following November. In 1988, Mrs. Mary James, the first African-American female to become a pastoral administrator in the Diocese of Cleveland, took over all daily responsibilities and business affairs of the parish. She served in that capacity until her retirement in July 1996.

The Mount Pleasant urban community and parish continued to struggle with problems common to the other urban churches within the Diocese. Most of the parish families moved away to the suburbs, and few of the newcomers to the neighborhood were Catholic.

Near the end, Epiphany was without a resident priest. Father Dan Begin, pastor of St. Cecilia Church, ended up doing double duty, providing sacramental service to both parishes. Epiphany closed its church doors on May 24, 2009.

The Thea Bowman Center continues. Located at the same site as Epiphany Church, it counts itself as a neighborhood safe haven. It offers art, music, a food pantry, summer lunch and Saturday hot meals, GED/adult basic education, academic tutoring, computer data training, 4H, and a wellness center offering blood pressure testing.

The Center hopes to continue reaching out to its neighborhood as it is much needed in the Mount Pleasant community. The urban 4H group at the Thea Bowman Center (TBC) spoke about the importance of these programs in their lives, and how the center is a place they have loved visiting after school. They want to make a difference in others' lives while the TBC makes a huge difference in theirs. It gives them a place to grow and learn the values of independence and self confidence, and more importantly it makes them aware of their own value to the local community.

Even with the sadness of Epiphany's closing, the doors of the Thea Bowman Center will remain open and continue to help and change people's lives and better the community at large.

Ss. Philip and James

BOSWORTH ROAD, CLEVELAND
FOUNDED: 1950
LAST MASS: MAY 3, 2010

ARCHITECTURE IS NOT IN THE EMPTY BUILDING, BUT IN THE VITAL
INTERCHANGE BETWEEN BUILDING AND PARTICIPANT. **CESAR PELLI**

ISHOP EDWARD F. HOBAN established the new parish of Ss. Philip and James on the occasion of their feast day, May 1, 1950. Fr. James O'Brien, at the time Diocesan Director of the Catholic Youth Organization, was named pastor of the fledging parish. The name for the new parish was a tribute to the new pastor and his brother, the late Fr. Philip J. O'Brien, who had been killed in an automobile accident in 1934.

Fr. O'Brien was a strong candidate for the daunting job of launching a new parish. He was not a novice to new ventures, however. When he started as director of the CYO program in 1937, it was a new program to Cleveland. By the time he began his pastorate at Ss. Philip and James, the CYO program had grown to include more than 125 active units, as well as annual summer camps.

Ss. Philip and James School opened in February 1951 with 270 students in the first through sixth grades. At the time of its opening, a railroad strike was in effect, which led to delays in window and desk deliveries. As a result, students used their laps as desks, and plastic wrapping kept out the winter cold. The Franciscan Sisters of Blessed Kunegunda were brought in to staff the school, along with three lay teachers.

The first Mass in the 780-seat church was held on Christmas 1951. Before that date, Masses had been celebrated in the school auditorium. The church and school buildings were constructed from Ohio sandstone at a total cost of $300,000.

Disaster struck the area in 1953 when a devastating tornado hit the neighborhood. For three days, the parish became a Red Cross shelter for victims. The 107th Armored Cavalry Regiment established its field headquarters at Ss. Philip and James.

The parish remained strong and active even with its setbacks. The parish had many active groups; the Women's Guild, the Altar and Rosary Society, Parent Teacher Unit, the Men's and Boy's Choir, and Choral Club, to name just a few.

Later, the parish reached out to the community with its Holy Name Society, St. Vincent DePaul Society, and Ancient Acolytes, along with several youth groups. The parish continued to grow, reaching a congregation of 1,600 households.

In 1963, faulty wiring caused a fire in the rectory, which spread to a home at 3673 Bosworth, resulting in $20,000 of damages. Following the fire, fundraising efforts allowed the parish to build a permanent home for the priests as well as a convent for the Franciscan Sisters. Both buildings were completed in 1964.

Fr. O'Brien's health began to decline in 1973, forcing him to retire the following year; he was named pastor emeritus July 1, 1974. To honor the founding pastor, the parish hall was dedicated in his name in October 1974. Sadly, Fr. O'Brien died only a few months later, on March 6, 1975, and Fr. Robert F. Brennan became the new pastor.

Like many other Cleveland parishes, Ss. Philip and James experienced a decline in membership through the 1970s and 1980s, as people moved out of the city and into the suburbs. The Franciscan Sisters left the school in 1981 and were replaced by the Sisters of the Humility of Mary, who had assisted the Franciscan nuns during previous years. In 1995, the Sisters of the Humility of Mary also left the school, leaving the convent vacant. Enrollment continued to drop and the school was forced to close in June 1998.

The third pastor at Ss. Philip and James was Fr. Brendan McNulty. Fr. McNulty strived to find ways to use the empty buildings to help the parish. In keeping with the outreach mission of the church, the convent was leased to a group of women seeking to convert it into a maternity home for girls in need of a safe haven. This was a bold, forward-thinking gesture on the part of the parish, but unfortunately the group of women could not secure the necessary funding, and their plans fell through.

In 1999, renovations began on the school to house the Horizon Science Academy for seventh, eighth, and ninth grade students.

The church continued to reach out to the neighborhood until its doors closed in May 2010.

Other Closed Churches

Six more churches were suppressed by the Diocese of Cleveland, and their doors were locked before it was possible to photograph their interiors. Those churches were:

ST. JOSEPH CHURCH
FOUNDED AS A GERMAN PARISH IN 1896
REED AVENUE AND 15TH STREET, LORAIN
LAST MASS, MARCH 7, 2010

SAINTS CYRIL AND METHODIUS CHURCH
FOUNDED AS A SLOVAK PARISH IN 1906
189 15TH STREET, BARBERTON
LAST MASS, JUNE 14, 2009

SACRED HEART OF JESUS CHURCH
FOUNDED AS A HUNGARIAN PARISH IN 1922
162 IRONDALE STREET, ELYRIA
LAST MASS, JUNE 29, 2009

ST. HEDWIG CHURCH
FOUNDED AS A POLISH PARISH IN 1912
213 EAST GLENWOOD AVENUE, AKRON
LAST MASS, JANUARY 26, 2009

SACRED HEART OF JESUS CHURCH
FOUNDED AS A HUNGARIAN PARISH IN 1915
734 GRANT STREET, AKRON
LAST MASS, JANUARY 21, 1910

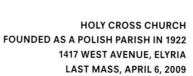

HOLY CROSS CHURCH
FOUNDED AS A POLISH PARISH IN 1922
1417 WEST AVENUE, ELYRIA
LAST MASS, APRIL 6, 2009

Epilog

"Let us build a house where love can dwell" are the opening words to the hymn "All are Welcome" by composer Mary Haugen. It beautifully describes the images presented in this book. Although we weep as the doors of so many "houses of God's love" are shuttered, the love and faith which built these places of prayer remain strong.

Debbie First has tried to capture that love in this, her first publication, and it is a true gift to the People of God in the Diocese of Cleveland. No words can clearly describe what these buildings meant to the many generations who had worshiped and passed on their faith within their walls, yet the photographs manage to evoke both feelings of celebration and sorrow as one views the statues and soaring arches which have inspired countless believers.

I hope that you have been able to view this book as a prayer of thanksgiving, one that expresses gratitude to God for those who have gone before us in faith. I also hope that you were able to celebrate the sacrifices of so many faithful people who made these buildings possible.

May each of us continue to believe that "wherever two or more are gathered in the name of the Jesus, God is found."

FATHER TOM FANTA
Pastor
Church of St. Dominic

Acknowledgments

Sources

Jim Toman and Cleveland Landmarks Press, Inc., for making this book happen, and for holding my hand every step of the way;

Tim Lachina and Walter Greene+Company, for their beautiful book design work;

Sister Rita Mary Harwood, SND and all at Parish Life and Development, for their endless support in this project;

Diana Medalie thank you for your help throughout this whole project, and your great friendship;

Christine Dziedzina, Phyllis and George Zindroski, Michele Dragas and her family;

Many thanks to Fr. Dan Begin, Fr. Gene Wilson, Fr. Tom Fanta, and Sr. Sheila Tobbe;

Gizella Becsei, Barb Zubricky, Mary Treese Slota and her family;

Kay Deininger, Norbert Hannibal, Janet Birtley, and all the women of the St. Francis class of 1952;

Lois Sever and the choir at St. Lawrence, and Judy and Chris Grozdanik;

Mary Jane Slomkowski and her whole beautiful family;

James Redford and Suzanne Nissim-Sabat Redford for all their help;

Many thanks to Jim Noga, Linda Carnivale, and the Our Lady of Mercy class of 1972; Sue Minoski and the Our Lady of Mercy class of 1970; and Ida Bodlor, Tom and Liz Walker, Barbara Ann Robinson, Lula Bell Williams, Thomas Williams, Tammy Jackson, and Linda Gamble.

People of Faith, Parishes and Religious Communities of the Diocese of Cleveland

St. Adalbert, "Diamond Jubilee", "A Historical Overview of the Founding of Our Lady of the Blessed Sacrament, St. Adalbert Church 2006"

"St. Barbara Church, 1905-2005"

Blessed Sacrament Church, "Diamond Celebration"

St. Casimir, "90th Anniversary Book," "Centennial Book"

St. Cecilia Church "50th Anniversary Book"

St. Emeric "Jubilee Anniversary Book"

Epiphany "50th Anniversary Book"

St. Francis Church, "1887-2009 Anniversary/History"

St. Hedwig Church, Lakewood "100 Year Anniversary Book"

St. Hyacinth "75th Diamond Jubilee Book," "100th Anniversary Book"

St. James "100th Anniversary Book," Guide to Stones used for Houses of Worship in North East Ohio, by Joseph T. Hannibal

St. Lawrence "85 Years of Ministry Book"

Historic St. Peter Church, "A Guide to the Church Interior and Furnishings"

St. Procop "Anniversary Book"

Saints Philip and James Church, "50th Anniversary Book"

Our Lady of Mercy, history and photographs are with great thanks to Jim Noga

St. Margaret of Hungary, "Diamond Jubilee Anniversary Book"

Sacred Heart of Jesus, "History Book"

St. Ladislaus, "A Century of Worship in the Spirit of our Hungarian Heritage"

St. Stanislaus, "100 Years Remembered"

St. Wendelin, "100th Anniversary"

STATUE DETAIL FROM BLESSED SCARAMENT CHURCH